Faith 4 Life

Senior High Bible Study Series

Sexuality

Group
Loveland, Colorado

Group's R.E.A.L. Guarantee to you:

This Group resource incorporates our R.E.A.L. approach to ministry—one that encourages long-term retention and life transformation. It's ministry that's:

Relational
Because learner-to-learner interaction enhances learning and builds Christian friendships.

Experiential
Because what learners experience through discussion and action sticks with them up to 9 times longer than what they simply hear or read.

Applicable
Because the aim of Christian education is to equip learners to be both hearers and doers of God's Word.

Learner-based
Because learners understand and retain more when the learning process takes into consideration how they learn best.

Faith 4 Life
SENIOR HIGH BIBLE STUDY SERIES

Sexuality

Visit our Web site: **www.grouppublishing.com**

Credits
Contributing Authors: David Cassady, Debbie Gowensmith, Ken and Lori Niles, Linda Snyder, and Helen Turnbull
Editor: Kelli B. Trujillo
Creative Development Editors: Mikal Keefer and Amy Simpson
Chief Creative Officer: Joani Schultz
Copy Editor: Loma Huh
Art Director: Sharon Anderson
Cover Art Director/Designer: Jeff A. Storm
Photographer: Daniel Treat
Print Production Artist: Stephen Beer
Production Manager: DeAnne Lear

ISBN 0-7644-2479-3

10 9 8 7 6 5 4 3 2 1 12 11 10 09 08 07 06 05 04 03

Printed in the United States of America.

CONTENTS

INTRODUCTION

SEXUALITY

"The Talk."

It's dreaded by adolescents. It's that traumatic and nightmarish moment when Mom or Dad sits down to tell them about...S-E-X.

For many, the prospect of discussing the topic in health class—or in youth group—can seem equally horrifying.

Yet, sex is *everywhere*. Teenagers are bombarded by sexual messages all the time through television, music, movies, billboards, magazines, clothing styles, the Internet, and more. And even those few teenagers who may somehow be miraculously protected from these negative influences still end up interacting with their peers; that interaction, in and of itself, can often be all it takes to trigger sexual questions and urges. After all, adolescents are virtual hormone hurricanes—their bodies are changing and they're experiencing desires and thoughts unlike anything they've felt before.

Teenagers are bombarded by sexual messages all the time through television, music, movies, billboards, magazines, clothing styles, the Internet, and more.

These four Bible studies will equip you to tackle critical issues related to sexuality as you lay a foundation for living by God's principles. In the first study, teenagers will closely examine Scripture and will discover that God is the creator of "good sex"—but that it is meant exclusively for the context of marriage. They'll come to understand that sexual intimacy creates a bond between two people: a bond that thrives only between a husband and a wife.

But living by that principle isn't always easy! In the second study, students will take a look at sexual temptation and will consider how they can stand by God's principles in the midst of enticing dating scenarios. They'll reflect on some of the consequences of acting on their sexual urges and will make practical commitments about "how far" they're willing to go in dating situations.

Students will then move into a discussion of sexual confusion and gender identity in Study 3. They'll scrutinize many of society's harmful messages about masculinity and femininity and will take a look at how those messages and other negative circumstances can lead people to become involved in sexual experimentation or to feel uncertain about their gender identity. Through a closer look at Scripture, teenagers will come to grasp the awesome truth that God can help people overcome these tough sexual identity issues through his amazing love.

The fourth Bible study will touch on another difficult issue: sexual victimization. It will help teenagers understand that God can enable them to forgive those who've hurt them and can heal the deep pain in their lives. Likewise, students who may have hurt others or who may feel guilty about sexual sins they've committed in the past will learn that God's forgiveness extends to them too!

Faith 4 Life: Sexuality will help you give teenagers a comprehensive look at God's intention for sexual expression. Through these four Bible studies, you'll use the light of God's truth to illuminate the often confusing and scary area of sexuality—and teenagers will discover that God's plan really is the best!

Senior High Bible Study Series

Faith 4 Life: Senior High Bible Study Series helps teenagers take a Bible-based approach to faith and life issues. Each book in the series contains these important elements:

- ***Life application of Bible truth***
  Faith 4 Life studies help teenagers understand what the Bible says and then apply that truth to their lives.
- ***A relevant topic***
  Each Faith 4 Life book focuses on one main topic, with four studies to give your students a thorough understanding of how the Bible relates to that topic. These topics were chosen by youth leaders as the ones most relevant for senior high students.
- ***One point***
  Each study makes one point, centering on that one theme to make sure students really understand the important truth it conveys. This point is stated upfront and throughout the study.
- ***Simplicity***
  The studies are easy to use. Each contains a "Before the Study" box that outlines any advance preparation required. Each study also contains a "Study at a Glance" chart so you can quickly and easily see what supplies you'll need and what each study will involve.
- ***Action and interaction***
  Each study relies on experiential learning to help students learn what God's Word has to say. Teenagers discuss and debrief their experiences in large groups, small groups, and individual reflection.
- ***Reproducible handouts***
  Faith 4 Life books include reproducible handouts for students. No need for student books!
- ***Tips, tips, and more tips***
  Faith 4 Life studies are full of "FYI" tips for the teacher, providing extra ideas, insights into young people, and hints for making the studies go smoothly.
- ***Flexibility***
  Faith 4 Life studies include optional activities and bonus activities. Use a study as it's written, or use these options to create the study that works best for your group.
- ***Follow-up ideas***
  At the end of each book, you'll find a section called "Changed 4 Life." This section provides ideas for following up with your students to make sure the studies stick with them.

Use Faith 4 Life studies to show your teenagers how the Bible is relevant to their lives. Help them see that God can invade every area of their lives and change them in ways they can only imagine. Encourage your students to go deeper into faith—faith that will sustain them for life! Faith 4 Life, forever!

SEX—WORTH WAITING FOR

Right now, about half of teenagers are doing it.

They're risking disease and pregnancy. But even if they avoid those consequences, there is one they can't avoid: a shattered heart.

Our sex-saturated society devalues and distorts one of God's greatest gifts. And many students have bought into the lie. They don't see their sexuality in all its God-given splendor; instead, they've settled for a cheaper version of "true love." And that choice is killing them, one encounter at a time.

This study exposes teenagers to a powerful picture of positive and healthy sexuality surrounded by respect, dignity, longevity, and exclusivity. It's "good sex," God's way.

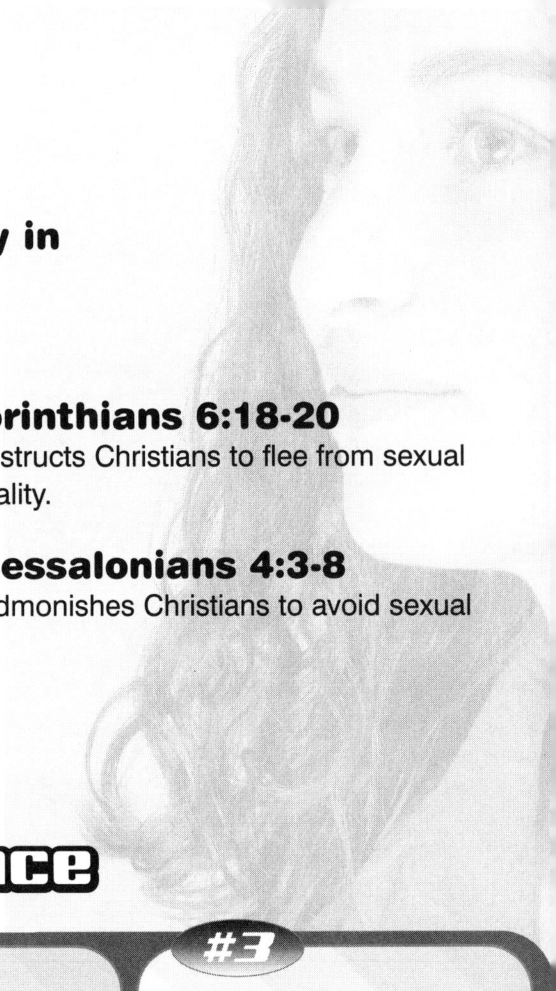

THE POINT

Sex creates a bond that thrives only in marriage.

SCRIPTURE SOURCE

Proverbs 5:3-8, 15-17
Solomon warns his sons not to have sex outside of marriage.

Song of Songs 4:1-7; 5:10-16
The man and woman in the story express how attracted they are to each other.

Song of Songs 8:6-7
The man in the story describes the amazing power of true love.

1 Corinthians 6:18-20
Paul instructs Christians to flee from sexual immorality.

1 Thessalonians 4:3-8
Paul admonishes Christians to avoid sexual sin.

THE STUDY AT A GLANCE

#1 For Starters
up to 15 minutes

■ BATTING PRACTICE

What students will do:
Choose words that define "good sex."

SUPPLIES:
- ❑ newsprint
- ❑ tape
- ❑ markers

■ BONUS ACTIVITY
up to 5 minutes

What students will do:
Choose words that describe their comfort levels when talking about sex.

SUPPLIES:
- ❑ pencils
- ❑ index cards

#2 Bible Truth
25-35 minutes

■ ROUNDING THE BASES

What students will do:
Form teams to search the Bible for the answer to the question "What is sex for?" and use a target to explain the environment in which sex thrives best.

SUPPLIES:
- ❑ newsprint
- ❑ tape
- ❑ markers
- ❑ Bibles
- ❑ index cards
- ❑ pencils

#3 Life Application
5-10 minutes

■ FOUL PLAY

What students will do:
Try to peel apart glued paper hearts without tearing the paper.

SUPPLIES:
- ❑ construction paper
- ❑ white glue
- ❑ pencils

***FYI**

This Bible study covers a sensitive topic: God's plan for sexual intimacy. It's a good idea to let parents know what you'll be studying so that they can both support you in your efforts and be prepared to discuss the topic further with their children if needed. Plan on scheduling a meeting for parents before you begin this series. At the meeting, present what you'll be covering in the various lessons and answer any questions parents may have. If parents have further questions, invite them to borrow this book and read through the Bible study material themselves.

***FYI**

If your group has fewer than nine people, have teenagers remain in one group to create all three lists. That will allow students to more effectively pool their creativity.

BEFORE THE STUDY

For the Bible Truth section, create a large version of the "Sex Target" (see diagram on p. 12) on a sheet of newsprint, and tape it to a wall. Also, gather several bottles of glue and enough pieces of construction paper so that each student can have two for "Foul Play."

FOR STARTERS

up to 15 minutes

BATTING PRACTICE

Say: Today we're going to talk about one of the hottest topics in the world. Advertisers use it to grab your attention. Musicians sing about it to shock or persuade you. Health class teachers talk about it in the classroom (much to their students' dismay). And parents discuss it with their students in one of the most dreaded of childhood or teenage experiences: "*The Talk*."

You guessed it. Today we're going to discuss sex.

In order to talk about sex, we must first agree on what positive or healthy sex is. Let's define positive or healthy sex by creating word lists that describe these key words: *love*, *sexuality*, and *respect*.

Have teenagers form three groups; then give each group a marker and a sheet of newsprint with one of the key words written at the top.

Say: In your group, create a list of synonyms and related words that describe your key word. For example, for *sexuality* you might list *intimacy* or *lust*. Please avoid writing down anything that others might find offensive. Go!

When each group has listed about ten words, have students select two words that best describe their key word and write them on a new sheet of newsprint taped to the wall. When this new list has been completed, **ask:**

- **What words from this list seem to be the most important for positive or healthy sex?**
- **Are there any words on this list that surprise you? Why or why not?**

- **Are there any words you would add or delete? Explain.**
- **How is our word picture of positive or healthy sex like or unlike the way society views sex? your peers view sex? you view sex? God views sex?**

Say: When you have sex without considering the importance of the key words we've listed here, sex becomes cheap and your relationships end up hurting you. Sex creates a bond that thrives only in marriage. We'll spend the rest of the study exploring that truth.

THE POINT

*FYI

The "love rationale" so prevalent in youth culture today claims that sex is OK if two people "really love each other." But what is love? How do you define it? Love is difficult for just about anyone to define, including your young people. So how can students know when they're really "in love"? For example, is it really love if it's based solely on emotion? Is it really love if it doesn't involve a lifetime commitment?

To help your teenagers gain a clear picture of what real love is all about, check out 1 Corinthians 13:1-8a. Challenge students to compare their concepts of love with the description in that passage; then they can see how deep their "love" relationships really go.

*FYI

As the teenagers create their lists, be sure they understand there are no right or wrong answers. Encourage them to think of as many words as possible. The longer their lists, the clearer the word picture will be.

BONUS ACTIVITY

up to 5 minutes

If you have time, use this activity before "Batting Practice" to help students warm up to the topic of discussion. Give each person an index card and a pencil. Tell students to write on their cards one word that describes how they feel when talking about sex. Provide examples of "feeling" words such as *uncomfortable*, *embarrassed*, *silly*, *confident*, or *excited*. Keep the responses anonymous to encourage teenagers to be honest.

Collect the cards, shuffle them, then ask the group to join you in prayer. **Pray:**

> **Lord, we want to learn from you today about our sexuality, but that can be difficult when confusing feelings get in the way. As we talk about this issue today, help us each deal with these emotions...**Read the cards aloud as part of your prayer, then **say: Thank you, Lord. In Jesus' name, amen.**

After the prayer, **say:**

> **Everyone has different feelings when talking about sex. As we warm up to the idea of sharing our feelings, remember to respect each other's ideas and listen to each other without put-downs or inappropriate humor.**

BIBLE TRUTH

25 to 35 minutes

ROUNDING THE BASES

Say: Now that we've decided what positive or healthy sex is about, let's see if we can answer the next question: "What is sex for?"

Form groups of three. Have each trio designate one person to be a one, one person to be a two, and one person to be a three. Give each person an index card, a pencil, and a Bible. Have all the ones write "Proverbs 5:3-8, 15-17" at the top of their cards. Have all the twos write "Song of Songs 4:1-7; 5:10-16; 8:6-7" at the top of their cards. Have all the threes write "1 Corinthians 6:18-20; 1 Thessalonians 4:3-8" at the top of their cards.

Assign each number a corner of the room. As soon as groups are in their respective corners, have students work together to write the **answer** to this question on their cards:

- **According to your assigned Scripture passages, what is sex for?**

While groups are working, be available to help students discover how their Scripture passages help answer the question "What is sex for?" Then, when all three sections have finished, have teenagers return to their trios. Starting with the ones, give each trio member one minute to teach the others what he or she learned.

Then **say:**

In the previous activity, we created a list of words describing positive and healthy sex. Now we've looked through Scripture to figure out exactly what sex is for. Here comes the real test.

Based on all your trio's information, write on the back of one of your cards a definition of positive and healthy sex. Your definition may not be longer than one sentence, and all three members must agree on it. You have two minutes. Go!

After two minutes, have each trio read its definition to the rest of the group. Then **say:**

Here's one more definition for you to consider: "Positive and healthy sex occurs only when two people share intimate love, trust, and respect in an exclusive, marriage relationship."

Repeat the definition, then **ask:**

***FYI**

If you have more than twenty students, have the teenagers in each corner form pairs. This will speed up the discussion time and allow everyone to participate.

***FYI**

Some group members may have trouble agreeing on what exactly constitutes sex. Is it "making out"? foreplay? sexual intercourse? all of these? If a debate arises, it may help to read definitions of sex from a dictionary.

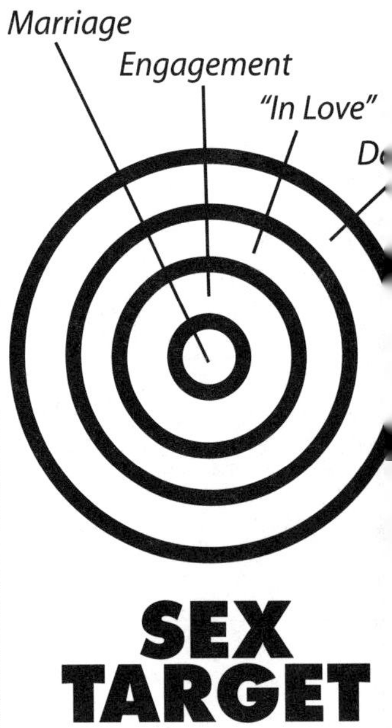

*FYI

If a group decides that sex outside of marriage is OK, ask these questions:

- Do you believe the Bible contains God's instructions for how we should live? Why or why not?
- How do you reconcile the fact that the Bible doesn't support your position on sex outside of marriage?
- How can you be certain that you're right and that God and the Bible are wrong?

- **What's your reaction to this definition?**
- **Do you believe that sex creates a bond that thrives only in marriage? Why or why not?** THE POINT

Say: Let's use your definitions of positive and healthy sex to decide whether sex really can thrive outside of marriage.

One at a time, have trios read aloud their definitions of positive and healthy sex and then tape them to the "Sex Target" you posted on the wall before the study. Have them put their definition where they think positive and healthy sex thrives best.

After all the trios have done this, **ask:**

- **What does this activity tell you about sex? about relationships?**
- **How does sex create a bond between two people?**
- **Why does the sexual bond thrive only in marriage?**
- **Why do you think God wants us to avoid sex outside of marriage?**

Say: Sex creates a bond that thrives only in marriage. We can choose to have sex outside of marriage, but when we do, we not only disobey God, we also hurt ourselves, our future spouses, and the people we have sex with. Sex is powerful. That's why God designed it to stay within the bounds of a marriage relationship. THE POINT

*FYI

As students study the relationship between the lovers in the Song of Songs, they might be tempted to interpret that relationship as permission to have sex outside of marriage. You can help your teenagers understand the true meaning of these passages by explaining these facts:

- The Song of Songs describes the love between a king and a Shulammite woman. The book follows the couple through the courtship, the wedding, and the married life that follows. Although the couple are in love from the beginning of the book, they do not consummate the relationship until after they're married.
- The term *lover* used in the Song of Songs doesn't mean "sexual partner" as it might today. Instead, it's simply a term of affection like *my love* or *my beloved.*

LIFE APPLICATION

5 to 10 minutes

FOUL PLAY

Set out several bottles of white glue, and give each person a sheet of construction paper and a pencil. Have each person tear two heart shapes out of the construction paper and glue the shapes together. Make sure students glue the edges of the sheet together. On each heart, have teenagers write one way having sex would bond them to another person. After a minute, ask volunteers to tell the group what they wrote. Then **say:**

Sex will create a bond, every time. God made sex to create a permanent bond between two people. Sex bonds us together just as our paper hearts are bonded together.

Have students set their paper hearts aside. Direct students to pray individually about their attitudes and desires concerning sex. Encourage students who have already had sex to pray for God's forgiveness and restoration. Challenge students who have not had sex to pray for God's strength to stand strong and for God to help their future spouses stand strong.

Have teenagers try to separate their two hearts without damaging them. Once all the hearts have been torn apart, **say:**

When we choose to have sex outside of marriage, the bond that sex creates rips us apart, sometimes even before the relationship is over. Sex creates a bond that thrives only in marriage. Outside of marriage, sex makes us look like this! THE POINT

Hold up one of the torn paper hearts.

Say: Take the paper heart home with you to serve as a reminder of what happens to your heart when you have sex outside of marriage. Strive for sexual and spiritual purity.

*FYI

Unless the students in your class defy the odds, several of them have likely already been involved in sexual behaviors. Be sensitive to this and spend some time talking about God's forgiveness and the healing power of the grace of Jesus Christ. Use the following passages to help you address the issue of forgiveness: 2 Samuel 11:1–12:13; Psalm 32; Psalm 51; Ephesians 2:1-10; and 1 John 1:9.

Also, be aware that some students in your group may have been victims of sexual abuse, rape, or other crimes. Take a moment to encourage students who may have an experience like this in their past to seek counseling. Also, be aware that the topic of victimization and forgiveness will be covered in greater detail in Study 4 (pp. 37-46).

DATING DILEMMAS

Knowledge doesn't always translate into action. Students may *know* that God intends for them to save sex until marriage, but that knowledge may do little to stop them from going "too far" when they're in the midst of a hot and heavy moment with a boyfriend or girlfriend. Hormonal urges are powerful! And when teenagers experience intense sexual desires in dating scenarios, it is often way too easy to set God's will aside in an effort to satisfy those desires.

This study will help teenagers think through some of the consequences of giving in to sexual temptation as they look at the bad choices David made when he encountered Bathsheba. They'll learn how important it is to set standards for physical behavior *before* they get into a tempting situation and will learn the importance of encouraging each other to make good decisions for dealing with desire.

THE POINT

It's important to set high standards for dealing with sexual desires.

SCRIPTURE SOURCE

2 Samuel 11:2-17
The writer describes the story of David and Bathsheba.

1 Corinthians 10:13
Paul explains that God helps us withstand temptation.

Proverbs 6:27-28
These verses discuss the inevitable consequences of our actions.

THE STUDY AT A GLANCE

#1 For Starters
up to 15 minutes

■ **WEIGHTY CHOICES**

What students will do:
Work together to tackle a "heavy" guessing game.

SUPPLIES:
- ❑ paper bags
- ❑ sealable plastic bags
- ❑ bathroom scale
- ❑ water
- ❑ paper
- ❑ pencil

#2 Bible Truth
20-30 minutes

■ **LOVE CONNECTION**

What students will do:
Experience how their actions affect others.

SUPPLIES:
- ❑ ball of yarn
- ❑ Bibles
- ❑ "Dealing With Desires: David's Dilemma" handout (p. 24)
- ❑ pens or pencils

#3 Life Application
10-15 minutes

■ **DATING STEAM-METER**

What students will do:
Set boundaries for their behavior in tempting situations.

SUPPLIES:
- ❑ "Dating Steam-Meter" handouts (p. 25)
- ❑ pencils

■ **BONUS ACTIVITY**
5-10 minutes

What students will do:
Brainstorm dating activities that avoid opportunities for sexual temptation.

SUPPLIES:
- ❑ paper
- ❑ pencils

*FYI

This Bible study covers a sensitive topic: dealing with sexual urges in dating situations. It's a good idea to let parents know what you'll be studying so that they can both support you in your efforts and be prepared to discuss the topic further with their children if needed. Plan on scheduling a meeting for parents before you begin this series. At the meeting, present what you'll be covering in the various lessons and answer any questions parents may have. If parents have further questions, invite them to borrow this book and read through the Bible study material themselves.

BEFORE THE STUDY

Before the study, prepare for "Weighty Choices" by pouring varying amounts of water into sealable small- to medium-sized plastic bags. Make sure any partially empty bags are inflated with air so they'll take up the same space as those filled with water. Place each plastic bag in a separate paper bag so students won't be able to tell how much the bags weigh by looking at them. Be sure to have at least ten bags for this activity. Line up the bags on a table. Set out a bathroom scale that can measure as little as two pounds.

FOR STARTERS

up to 15 minutes

WEIGHTY CHOICES

Begin by pointing out the paper bags and the scale. **Say:**

In a moment, you'll work together to see who can identify how many bags it takes to reach a weight of two pounds. Here's how it works: When it's your turn to guess, you must choose which bags you'll place on the scale. You can select as many or as few bags as you'd like. Once you touch a bag, you must use it. You may place the bags on the scale only after you've chosen all the bags you're going to use. Your goal is to get as close to two pounds as possible without going over the two-pound limit.

Ask for a volunteer who'd like to try the challenge first. Encourage the volunteer to get input from the other students while he or she is selecting bags. After the volunteer has attempted it, have him or her return the paper bags to the table. Continue having students take turns choosing bags and placing them on the scale, and keep track of each participant's final weight. (Warn students not to be rough with the bags or you'll have a disaster on your hands!) As participants choose the bags they want, encourage them to "take just one more."

After everyone has had a chance to try this challenge or after about seven minutes, congratulate the student who, with the help of the group, got the closest to two pounds without going over. Then **ask** everyone:

- **How did you feel during this game?**

*FYI

Add extra laughs to this game by using a noisemaker of some kind whenever students go over the two-pound limit. For example, you could use a buzzer from a board game, a bicycle horn, or even a clanging gong.

- What was your strategy?
- How tempting was it to take "just one more" bag? Explain.

Say: Dealing with sexual desires in dating can be a lot like this activity. We will often set a limit for our physical behavior, but then we try to get as close to that limit as possible. Likewise, it's easy to end up going over our limits without intending to.

Ask:
- How else is this game similar to sex and dating?
- How was the temptation to take "just one more" bag similar to the temptation to explore sex in dating?
- Why do people who are dating feel pressure to explore and act on their sexual feelings?

Say: God wants us to reserve sex for marriage, but that's not easy to do when you face sexual temptations in dating. When two people date, they become closer in many ways. And the pressure to give in to sexual desires becomes stronger and stronger over time. Dealing with those desires isn't easy, and sometimes people make decisions they later regret. The Bible shows us that **it's important to set high standards for dealing with sexual desires.** Let's take a closer look at a biblical example we can learn a lot from.

THE POINT

*NOTES

BIBLE TRUTH

20 to 30 minutes

LOVE CONNECTION

Ask: What do you know about David in the Bible? Describe what kind of person he was.

If students need help, remind them that David was an incredible leader and a man who loved God very much. Point out that he wrote many of the psalms in the Bible and he was even called a man after God's own heart.

Have teenagers form small groups of three to six students, and give each group a copy of "Dealing with Desires: David's Dilemma" (p. 24) and pens or pencils. Invite them to read 2 Samuel 11:2-17 in their groups and then work together to create a simple plot map on the handout, indicating the major events of the story. To create a plot map, teenagers should simply draw a straight line across the paper with squares along the line, indicating the main events of the story.

Invite students to **discuss** these questions in their small groups:

- **What did David do wrong in this story? Be specific.**
- **Why do you think he did each of those things?**
- **What could he have done differently?**

Instruct teenagers to draw an alternate plot map, showing what might have happened if David had dealt with his sexual desires differently. Encourage them to imagine and note positive situations that could have resulted if David had never chosen to seduce Bathsheba. To create this alternate map, they should branch off from the first event and draw a line parallel to their first plot map, adding squares indicating what would have been different.

When groups are done, invite them to explain what they created, then **ask:**

- **What were the consequences of David's choices?**
- **How were others affected by David's actions?**
- **How might things have been different if David had handled his sexual desires in a different way?**

Say: Even David, who loved God passionately, who was successful, and who was wise, fell prey to the power of his own sexual desires. Like David, we're not invincible when it comes to dating and desire—we, too, can very easily make wrong choices that will affect our lives in huge ways.

Invite a volunteer to read aloud Proverbs 6:27-28.

Ask:
- **How does this passage apply to dating and sex?**
- **Why is it important to set high standards for dealing with sexual desires in dating?**
- **What are some of the potential personal consequences of going too far sexually in a dating relationship?**
- **How can bad sexual choices in dating affect other people in your life besides yourself and your boyfriend or girlfriend?**

THE POINT

Say: When we make choices, we must be ready for the consequences. But consequences of poor sexual choices don't only affect the people making the decisions. David may have been ready to deal with the choices he made, but what about the effect his choice had on Bathsheba? And what about Uriah, who eventually died because of David's choices? An essential part of making good decisions about dating and sex is to remember that your actions affect other people.

Have teenagers stand in a circle. Invite a volunteer (an adult helper or a student) to use the ball of yarn by weaving it in between and around the students to "tie them up" as you read aloud the following sentences. Pause as necessary to allow enough time for the volunteer to completely entangle the teenagers during your talk.

Say: Imagine that you're on a date and things start getting physical. You know messing around sexually before marriage is risky, but you think, "Hey, it's my life and my decision." Yet before you act on this thought, the faces of people you know start forming in your mind. And in your heart, lines are drawn to

...people who trust your judgment;
...people you love and who love you;
...your parents;
...your grandparents;
...your Christian friends;
...your favorite teachers;
...your youth leaders at church;
...your future husband or wife;
...Jesus.

When teenagers are connected in several directions, **say:**

Look at the love lines connecting us, and think about all the ways we connect with people outside this room. Sex is a deeply personal gift; it changes us when we

NOTES

share it. And when we change, it affects all the other relationships in our lives. If people spread rumors, a partner feels used, a pregnancy occurs, or a disease is spread, others are even more deeply affected.

Ask:

- **How do you feel about being connected with the yarn?**
- **How is this like the way people feel when they consider the consequences of sexual involvement?**

Say: The next time you're tempted to give in to sexual desires on a date, remember that you're "all tied up" in lines of love—and that the consequences you might face affect more then just two people.

Have students untangle themselves and return to their seats.

*FYI

Students may have a variety of opinions about Bathsheba and her role in the events that took place. Some may place much of the blame for what happened on her while others may see both David and Bathsheba as equally responsible for what took place. Second Samuel doesn't give us a glimpse into what Bathsheba was thinking or feeling—we only know that she was summoned by the king and she did what he wanted.

Though Bathsheba certainly could have made other choices, you may want to remind students that women didn't have as much decision-making power in those days as they do now, and refusing a king's request was probably a pretty risky choice. It is entirely possible that Bathsheba did not want to have sexual relations with King David, but she did so because of cultural and political pressures. Help students think more deeply about these possibilities by asking:

- What do you think Bathsheba was thinking and feeling when she was summoned to the palace?
- What might she have thought or felt when David wanted to sleep with her?
- Do you think David was abusing his power in this situation? Why or why not?

LIFE APPLICATION

10 to 15 minutes

DATING STEAM-METER

Invite a volunteer to read aloud 1 Corinthians 10:13. **Say:**

No matter how strong your desires are or how tempted you feel, God will always provide you with a way to withstand those temptations. One of the best ways to deal with those situations is to set high standards for dealing with sexual desires in dating. ‹THE POINT

Give teenagers each a pencil and a "Dating Steam-Meter" handout (p. 25). **Say:**

Use this handout to help you think about when things start to get "out of control" in a physical relationship. You won't need to show this to anyone. When you're done, read and sign the commitment at the bottom of the page. Then find a partner and encourage him or her to act responsibly on dates; for example, say, "God will keep you strong when you're tempted" or "You can overcome the temptation to go too far." Take a moment to pray with your partner for wisdom in your dating decisions.

*FYI

Some of the students in your group may have never been in a sexually tempting situation; some of them may have never even been on a date. Sometimes students like this can begin to feel rather depressed during a discussion about dating, wondering why they haven't had some of the experiences their peers have had. They may also feel a bit awkward thinking about sexually tempting situations. Encourage these teenagers to take confidence in the standards they're setting and work hard to give them a self-esteem boost if needed. After all, in this area and with this age group, there's *nothing* wrong with a little naivete!

*FYI

Some students in your group may have already experienced the full range of activities on the "Dating Steam-Meter." When asked to draw a line on the meter setting standards for their actions, they may feel ashamed and unsure of what to do. Can they really start over and set their standards higher? Encourage students to remember that God is a God of new beginnings! The promise in 1 Corinthians 10:13 is meant for them, whether they've made mistakes in the past or not. God can give them the strength and wisdom needed to start new patterns of behavior. It won't be easy, though! Tell teenagers that you're available to talk with any of them who need some extra encouragement in this area of their lives.

BONUS ACTIVITY

5 to 10 minutes

101 IDEAS

If you have time, use this additional activity at the end of the study.

Say: The key to avoiding tempting sexual situations is to avoid dates that would easily lend themselves to "getting physical," such as going to a romantic movie or watching television together in an otherwise empty house.

Form groups of no more than five. Give groups each a sheet of paper and a pencil. Have groups each list dating activities that avoid opportunities for sexual involvement.

After a few minutes, have groups share what they brainstormed. Ask teenagers to commit to dating activities such as those listed and to stay away from activities that will tempt them sexually. Have volunteers close in prayer, asking for God's guidance in issues of sex and dating.

DEALING WITH DESIRES

DAVID'S DILEMMA

INSTRUCTIONS:
Create a plot line based on what happened in 2 Samuel 11:2-17. Simply draw a straight line across the paper and draw squares along the line, indicating the major events of the story.

David feels sexually tempted when he sees Bathsheba

Dating Steam-Meter

The closer you get to someone physically, the more tempted you are to "go further." And when you're in the heat of the moment, it's never easy to set limits on your physical relationship. Many times, people let their hormones guide them into sexual involvement, only to later feel regret or guilt for their hasty actions.

On the meter below, mark what your physical limits will be based on how you'd like to deal with sexual desires in a way that honors God. Be honest. No one will see your answers. Then, seriously evaluate your physical limitations by completing the questions below.

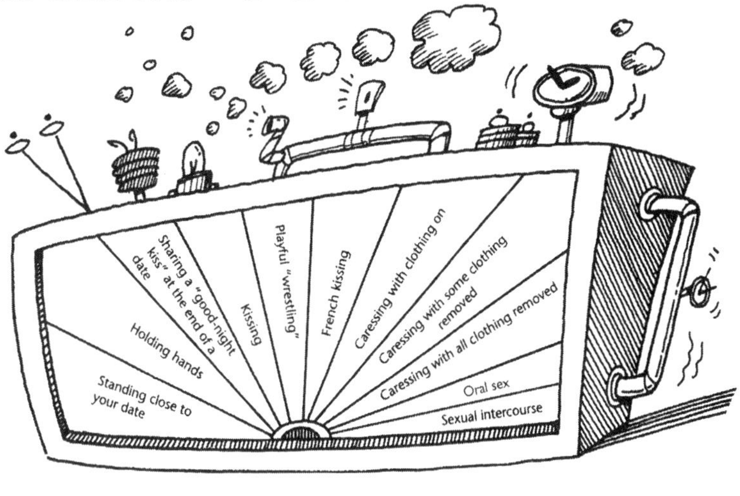

Answer the following questions:

- Is it easy to limit the physical aspect of a dating relationship? Why or why not?
- What is an appropriate limit for sexual activity in dating?
- How would God feel about the limit you've chosen on the Dating Steam-Meter?

Complete the following sentences:

- I date [or want to date] because:
- One thing I'll do to avoid sexual temptation in dating is:
- When I look at my mark on the Dating Steam-Meter, I feel:

Commitment:

I commit to follow God's will in my dating. I'll talk with other Christians when I have doubts about what's OK or not OK in my dating relationships. I'll seek guidance on proper limits of physical expression. And if I've already made sexual mistakes, I'll ask God to help me start over.

Signature: ______________________________

STRAIGHT AND NARROW?

In recent years, sex has moved from one of the most private of topics to the most public. It has become the major hook for advertising campaigns and television ratings wars. Sex is linked to everything from cars to toothpaste. And just when students experience the full barrage of sexuality from media, they are also confronted with the challenge of their own hormones.

Contrary to the changes in our society stand the sexual ethics of the Bible: God created us male and female, and the only proper expression of sexual intimacy is in the context of marriage. Unfortunately, this message has not always been clearly communicated in the church or integrated into the standards held by our youth.

During adolescence, teenagers' feelings of insecurity about who they are becoming and insecurity about how they measure up to the stereotypes of masculinity and femininity presented in the media often lead to sexual experimentation. Since sex is no longer a private issue, this experimentation and exploration can lead to practices and labels that cause students great pain.

This study will help your teenagers make some sense of the feelings and needs that surround sexual identity. It will help them understand that they can overcome temptation, change behavior, and live a pure life through God's grace.

THE POINT

God created us male and female.

SCRIPTURE SOURCE

Genesis 1:27; 2:18, 23-24
God created us male and female.

Matthew 11:28-30
Jesus provides rest for us.

John 8:34-36
Jesus sets us free.

1 Corinthians 6:9-11
God can forgive and change the lives of those involved in sin.

THE STUDY AT A GLANCE

#1 For Starters

15-20 minutes

■ **COVER SHOT**

What students will do:
Make magazine covers that demonstrate what it means to be male and female.

SUPPLIES:
- ❑ newsprint
- ❑ magazines
- ❑ scissors
- ❑ glue
- ❑ markers

■ **OPTIONAL ACTIVITY**
15-20 Minutes

What students will do:
Share their opinions on gender traits by participating in a physical activity.

#2 Bible Truth

25-30 minutes

■ **WHERE DO WE TURN?**

What students will do:
Generate lists of basic needs, then create necklaces that demonstrate the sins listed in 1 Corinthians 6:9-11 that they struggle with.

SUPPLIES:
- ❑ Bibles
- ❑ pens
- ❑ paper
- ❑ newsprint
- ❑ tape
- ❑ colored markers
- ❑ yarn
- ❑ index cards

#3 Life Application

5-10 minutes

■ **FREE INDEED**

What students will do:
Pray for each other and remove the necklaces from the "Where Do We Turn?" activity.

SUPPLIES:
- ❑ Bibles
- ❑ trash can

BEFORE THE STUDY

Take some time to prepare the supplies you'll need before the study begins. For "Cover Shot," you'll need to collect magazines, newsprint, glue, scissors, and markers. You'll need enough so that each group of four students can have two sheets of newsprint, at least two magazines, at least one pair of scissors and one bottle of glue, and at least one marker.

For the Bible Truth section, you'll need to prepare four sheets of newsprint. Write one of the following categories at the top of each sheet: physical, emotional, social, and spiritual. Write the numbers 1 through 10 down the left side of each sheet. Gather enough index cards so that each student can have one. Finally, cut enough 24-inch pieces of yarn so that you'll have one for each teenager.

***FYI**

This Bible study covers a sensitive topic: gender identity and sexual confusion. It's a good idea to let parents know what you'll be studying so that they can both support you in your efforts and be prepared to discuss the topic further with their children if needed. Plan on scheduling a meeting for parents before you begin this series. At the meeting, present what you'll be covering in the various lessons and answer any questions parents may have. If parents have further questions, invite them to borrow this book and read through the Bible study material themselves.

FOR STARTERS

15 to 20 minutes

COVER SHOT

After teenagers arrive, have them form groups of four. Give each group two sheets of newsprint, magazines, scissors, glue, and markers. **Say:**

> **Every day we see media images of what a "real" man or woman looks like and how he or she interacts with others. Using the supplies I've given you, create the covers of two separate magazines. One magazine should be titled "I Am Man." Your magazine cover should demonstrate what your group thinks a man *should* be like. For example, if a man should be sensitive, you could include a cover blurb that says something like "Get in touch with your sensitive side, page 8." Your other magazine should be titled "I Am Woman." This magazine should demonstrate what your group thinks a woman *should* be like.**
>
> **Carefully consider everything you put on your covers, making sure everything demonstrates what a man or woman should be.**

Give groups about seven minutes. Then **say:**

> **On the back of your "I Am Man" cover, make a list of all the inappropriate or confusing models of men we**

NOTES

see in society. For example, you could list things like "violent" or "uncaring." On the back of your "I Am Woman" cover, make a list of inappropriate or confusing models of women. For example, you could list "unintelligent" or "vengeful."

Have each group present its covers and lists. Then **ask:**

- **What similarities did you notice between the covers?**
- **How do the covers demonstrate the differences between males and females?**
- **Which elements do you think relate more to culture than to actually being male or female?**
- **What did your group base its concept of male and female images on?**
- **Were there some elements represented as being "good" or "bad" that really made you irritated or uncomfortable? Explain.**

Say: Think about where you would stand if I asked you to stand beside the cover that comes closest to representing you.

Ask:
- **Do any of these covers explain the whole story of who you are? Explain.**
- **What kinds of sexual labels does society put on men and women?**

Say: During this lesson, we're going to talk about sexual identity. We'll discuss how we can get "stuck" in distortions of God's design for our sexual identities and how we can get "unstuck" from unhealthy behaviors. We'll also look at how the fact that God created us male and female affects our sexuality. THE POINT

OPTIONAL ACTIVITY

15 to 20 minutes

Instead of "Cover Shot," try this optional activity.

Have students gather in the middle of the room and **say:**

Every day we see and hear messages that try to define what it means to be a man or what it means to be a woman.

Ask: What are some sources of these types of messages?

Explain that everyone will now have a chance to decide what they think about some of those messages and to see how their opinions line up with those of their peers. Tell students that you are going to mention several activities and traits, and it will be their job to determine if they think what you've said is masculine, feminine, or neutral. Designate one wall of the room as the "masculine" side, the other as the "feminine" side, and the middle as the "neutral" or "both masculine and feminine" area. Prompt teenagers to express their opinion by quickly moving to the area of their choice after each statement.

Say: In a moment, you're going to have a chance to vote on twenty different traits, but first let me encourage you to vote based on the way you *normally* think about these things in your everyday life, not just what you think you *should* vote for. In other words, if there are stereotypes about men or women that are commonly accepted and are generally part of the way you view things, then be honest and vote that way.

If students don't have any questions, begin the activity. **Say:**

A person who

...enjoys cooking and sewing (pause for students to select their corner)

...is addicted to video games (pause)

...loves sports (pause)

...is very religious (pause)

...enjoys reading and writing poetry (pause)

***FYI**

Some sources of gender messages that you may want to mention (if students don't) are television shows, magazines, songs, billboards, and music videos. Other powerful sources of messages are parents, family members, and friends.

...wears deodorant (pause)
...wears make-up (pause)
...enjoys babysitting (pause)
...is aggressive (pause)
...is shy (pause)
...studies ballet (pause)
...is violent (pause)
...wants to be a doctor (pause)
...wants to be a boxer (pause)
...is interested in fashion (pause)
...is kind (pause)
...excels in math and science (pause)
...loves singing (pause)
...enjoys fixing cars (pause)
...is emotional

Gather everyone back together and **ask:**

- **Which traits seemed to get the most "masculine" votes? "feminine" votes? "neutral" votes?**
- **What other traits or characteristics does society usually attribute to men? to women?**
- **What common stereotypes about masculinity and femininity are inappropriate, incorrect, or confusing?**
- **What are some of the negative effects of those stereotypes?**
- **Which elements of "masculinity" and "femininity" do you think relate more to culture than to actually being male or female?**
- **Do any of the traits we've discussed explain the whole story of who you are? Explain.**
- **What kinds of sexual labels does society put on men and women?**

Say: During this study, we're going to talk about sexual identity. We'll discuss how we can get "stuck" in distortions of God's design for our sexual identities, and how we can get "unstuck" from unhealthy behaviors. We'll also look at how the fact that God created us male and female affects our sexuality. THE POINT

BIBLE TRUTH

25 to 30 minutes

WHERE DO WE TURN?

Have students form same-sex groups of four. Give each group a pen and a sheet of paper.

Say: Fold your paper into fourths, then open the sheet. Put one of the following headings on each quarter: physical, emotional, social, and spiritual. In each of your groups, come up with a list of the most important needs you think people of your gender have in each category. For example, under the "physical" heading you could write "food" or "sleep."

After about five minutes, **say:**

If you haven't already, please include "same-gender friendships" in the appropriate place on your list.

Have each group rank the items in each category from most important to least important. While groups work, tape to the wall the four sheets of newsprint you prepared before the study. Designate one color of marker to be used by the male groups and one to be used by the female groups. Then have a representative from each group list its needs in order on the sheets of newsprint.

Ask:

- **What differences do you see between male and female needs on these lists?**
- **What other notable differences can you think of?**
- **What happens when individuals don't fall within those stereotypes? For example, a guy who is more concerned with** (the first item from one of the girl lists) **or a girl who is more concerned with** (the first item from one of the guy lists)**?**
- **How can these needs affect a person's sexual identity?**
- **How could negative feedback about feelings or needs affect someone's sexual identity?**

Say: The experience of negative feedback is one of the things that causes sexual confusion for people. When someone continually hears that his or her responses are not masculine enough or not feminine enough, that person can begin to doubt his or her identity.

Another source of confusion comes from not having good modeling of same-sex and other-sex relationships. For example, a person can become confused because of the modeling his or her parents gave.

NOTES

Ask: ■ **What other things can cause sexual confusion?**

■ **How should a person deal with sexual confusion?**

Say: The way individuals process or work through their sexual confusion depends on many factors. These factors include how secure they feel with themselves and their dependence on outside sources of authority, such as the Bible. Let's look at who we were created to be, according to the Bible.

Have volunteers read Genesis 1:27; 2:18; and 2:23-24 aloud.

Ask: ■ **What do these verses tell us about males and females?**

■ **What's the difference you see between the two?**

■ **Does this passage apply to *all* males and females? Explain.**

Say: The Bible gives a degree of freedom in our sexual identity. However, the Bible also demonstrates that God created us male and female and that our sexual purpose is fulfilled in the relationship of marriage. THE POINT

Say: When our needs aren't being fulfilled or when our understanding of our needs gets warped, we may turn to things for satisfaction that don't please God. Let's take a few minutes to look at what types of things people turn to.

Give each student a length of yarn, an index card, and a pen. Read 1 Corinthians 6:9-11 aloud.

Ask: How does this passage relate to the sexual confusion in our society today?

Say: First Corinthians 6:11 explains that some of the Christians in Corinth struggled with the sins listed. However, Christ cleansed and forgave them. I'd like you to spend some time looking at and thinking about 1 Corinthians 6:9-11. Which of the actions that Paul listed have you struggled with? Select at least one. Write the sin or sins on your index card—what you write will be kept private, just between you and God. With your pen, poke holes in the corners of your index card, and use the yarn to make your card into a necklace. Make sure your sin faces your chest rather than out. You may want to put the card inside your shirt so others won't see what you wrote.

Ask: ■ **How does it feel to wear your sin around your neck?**

■ **How would you feel if I asked you to turn the cards outward?**

- How would you want people to react to your necklace? your sin?
- How should we treat people who are struggling with one or more of the sins listed in 1 Corinthians 6:9-10? Explain.
- How can people find freedom from the sins listed in 1 Corinthians 6:9-10?
- Why do you think Paul lists all these sins together?
- How can confusion be a cause of these sins? a result?
- Is one sin on this list any worse than any other?

Say: God can forgive every sin. God can meet every unmet need. God can heal any lifestyle. God made us male and female. God knows our needs and weaknesses. He loves people who struggle with sexual immorality, homosexuality, greed, and all other types of sin. God also wants to set all people free through the forgiveness and cleansing that comes through Jesus Christ.

THE POINT

*NOTES

*FYI

What should you do if a teenager wants to talk to you about his or her struggles with homosexuality? First, the very fact that a teenager comes to you with this problem is a good sign. You are trusted. Work with the student to discover *all* the factors involved in his or her struggle.

The teenager needs to know that homosexuality is a changeable orientation. The world is telling him or her that there is no hope for change. While the scientific community searches for validation of "genetic predisposition" to homosexuality, hundreds of individuals offer personal empirical evidence that their lives have been changed. Your student needs to hear that there is hope in Christ. Back up the hope you share with Scripture relating to God's willingness to change lives. A good example is the story of the Samaritan woman (John 4:4-26) who also struggled with a sexually impure lifestyle.

The one thing adolescents fear most is rejection or being treated differently because of what they've shared. You can best help a student by following Jesus' example. Jesus associated with people in sin, and he loved them. We can do no less. You can also assure this individual of your respect for his or her willingness to honestly address the struggle as you talk and pray together.

Lastly, be careful not to overestimate your own counseling abilities. Whenever you feel "over your head" in a counseling situation, don't hesitate to refer a teenager to a professional Christian counselor.

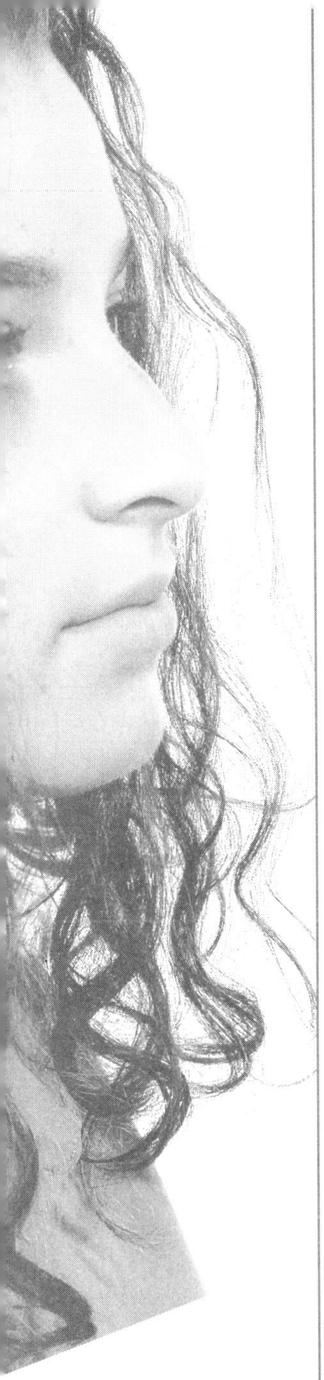

LIFE APPLICATION

5 to 10 minutes

FREE INDEED

Have teenagers form pairs. Ask pairs to read 1 Corinthians 6:11 again. Have pairs **discuss:**

- **What does it mean to be washed? sanctified? justified?**
- **How have you experienced one or more of those actions in your own life?**
- **How can you help others experience those actions?**

Read Matthew 11:28-30. **Ask:**

- **How does this passage apply to sexual confusion? to sin?**
- **How should Christians deal with sexual confusion they have? that others have?**

Say: I'd like you to pray with your partner about the sin you wrote on your card or another sin you're dealing with. You don't need to name the sin to your partner—you can speak generically if you'd like. Ask for God's forgiveness, cleansing, and power to change. If you're struggling with sexual confusion issues and would like someone to talk to, please feel free to talk to me after the meeting or call me tomorrow.

After students pray, have students remove their partner's necklaces (without reading the sin written on the card) and throw them away as you read John 8:34-36 aloud.

Say: Since God created us male and female, he understands all our needs—including those that relate to sexuality. He is able to set you free from any sin. It may take time until you see freedom, but the freedom will be complete. THE POINT

*FYI

Teenagers may have additional questions about homosexuality as a result of this study. Here are some common questions you may encounter and suggestions for answering students' concerns.

- *Are people born gay?*

Some scientific studies appear to indicate a genetic predisposition to homosexuality while other studies refute those findings. Though research continues to be done on this issue, no study has yet proven beyond doubt that there is a genetic cause of homosexuality nor a specific area of the brain or body that determines sexual orientation.

- *What causes someone to be homosexual?*

There are many psychological and social pressures that can contribute to a person's choices regarding sexual expression. Some of the best theories come from gay and formerly gay individuals themselves. Many people list one or a combination of the following causes: sexual abuse or experiences that mar perceptions of sexuality; inability to connect to same-sex friends, especially in critically formative periods of life; insecurity in gender roles leading to definition of sexual identity through sexual contact; and family relationships that don't encourage close connections.

Often these and other factors lead a particular individual to experiment with homosexual behavior in an attempt to deal with these pressures. Out of that experimentation, habits are formed and identities are established.

- *Can homosexuals change?*

Many formerly gay individuals would offer a resounding "Yes!" and show a lifestyle change that demonstrates it. At the same time, however, this radical change is not an easy one for others who do continue to struggle with homosexual urges throughout their life, though they choose not to act on them.

- *What can I do if a friend of mine is homosexual?*

You can pray and continue to be a friend! Your own identity does not need to be threatened by your friend's choices. Let your friend know that there are alternatives, but no one can change anything in his or her life unless there is personal commitment behind it. It's not your job to change your friend or to take responsibility for his or her choices.

- *If I have feelings for someone of the same sex, does that make me homosexual?*

No. It's normal to experience fleeting attraction to someone of the same sex. Recognizing that someone is attractive does not need to be interpreted as a sexual response. If you're experiencing sexual feelings that are uncomfortable for you or thoughts that are consuming too much emotional energy, it may help to seek the wisdom of a counselor or a mature Christian who can help you from a biblical point of view. Experimenting with sexual fantasies or behavior is not a healthy alternative.

VICTIMIZED

Sometimes forgiveness is easy. A person makes a mistake that hurts you. The offender apologizes, and you forgive him or her. What's done is done. You move on.

But forgiveness isn't always that straightforward, especially when it comes to sexual issues. In cases such as sexual abuse or sexual harassment, forgiveness can be *extremely* difficult. This kind of hurt leaves scars that can last a lifetime—psychological, emotional, or even physical scars. Sometimes the offender may not ever acknowledge that what he or she did was wrong. Can you forgive someone who does not ask for forgiveness? Are certain crimes so horrible that even God can't forgive them?

And what about students who've been "offenders" themselves—who've sexually victimized others or who feel wracked by guilt over some of their own past sexual behaviors or sexual thoughts? Is it possible to forgive oneself and experience healing from situations like these?

Statistics tell us that sexual victimization is much more common than we often realize; it is not an issue we should be silent about.

This study cannot teach students how to heal from deep wounds suffered as victims in any situation—it cannot provide a pat, pretty, fail-safe system on how to forgive and forget. Instead, this study can challenge teenagers to move beyond a superficial understanding of forgiveness. Through this Bible study, teenagers will discover that forgiveness is a long journey—one through which a God full of grace and love will help them travel.

THE POINT

God can provide healing and forgiveness for past hurts.

SCRIPTURE SOURCE

Genesis 37:18-28; 50:15-21
Joseph's brothers sold him into slavery; he later forgave them for mistreating him.

Isaiah 55:7
God promises to freely forgive those who come to him.

Luke 15:11-32
Jesus used the parable of the prodigal son to teach about God's forgiveness.

THE STUDY AT A GLANCE

#1 For Starters
10-15 minutes

■ **FORGIVENESS FEUD**

What students will do:
Play a game to uncover their attitudes toward forgiveness.

SUPPLIES:
- ❑ Bibles
- ❑ index cards
- ❑ pens or pencils

#2 Bible Truth
20-25 minutes

■ **CHAT ROOM**

What students will do:
Create a "chat room" to discuss sexual abuse and other kinds of victimization, and explore Scripture to learn about forgiveness.

SUPPLIES:
- ❑ Bibles
- ❑ chairs
- ❑ pens or pencils
- ❑ "NetTalk" handouts (p. 46)

#3 Life Application
15-20 minutes

■ **FORGIVENESS TRAIL**

What students will do:
Follow a masking tape trail while they learn that forgiveness is a process.

SUPPLIES:
- ❑ masking tape
- ❑ marker
- ❑ newsprint
- ❑ pens or pencils

■ **BONUS ACTIVITY**
up to 5 minutes

What students will do:
Symbolically express their desire to experience healing and forgiveness.

SUPPLIES:
- ❑ strips of construction paper
- ❑ staplers

*FYI

This Bible study covers a sensitive topic: sexual victimization. It's a good idea to let parents know what you'll be studying so that they can both support you in your efforts and be prepared to discuss the topic further with their children if needed. Plan on scheduling a meeting for parents before you begin this series. At the meeting, present what you'll be covering in the various lessons and answer any questions parents may have. If parents have further questions, invite them to borrow this book and read through the Bible study material themselves.

BEFORE THE STUDY

For the "Chat Room" activity, make one photocopy of the "NetTalk" handout (p. 46) for every student. Cut apart the three messages.

For the "Forgiveness Trail" activity, use masking tape to create a trail in one area of your room. Start at one end of the room, and finish at the opposite end. In between, create a haphazard path that twists and crosses over itself. Use a marker to denote five points along the way, using a "1" for the first point, a "2" for the second, and so on. You can vary the distance between these five points, but make sure there's enough distance for a group of four to fit between numbers.

Next create a corresponding sign for each point using five pieces of newsprint. Write one of these numbered steps on each piece of newsprint:

1. *In prayer, ask God to help you heal and forgive.*
2. *Confront the anger and resentment you feel; find a healthy way to release the anger.*
3. *View the offender as a human being, not a stereotype; identify with—not excuse—the offender to gain compassion.*
4. *Recognize that you need forgiveness sometimes and that Jesus forgives the offender.*
5. *Allow an internal, emotional release of pain and anger.*

(These steps adapted from Suzanne Freedman et al., "Five Points on the Construct of Forgiveness Within Psychotherapy," Psychotherapy, Fall 1991.)

Hang the pieces of newsprint in random order around the room, and place a pile of pens or pencils underneath each piece.

If you decide to do the Bonus Activity, cut sheets of construction paper lengthwise into 1-inch-wide strips. You'll need one strip for each teenager. You'll also need a stapler or multiple staplers for a large group.

*FYI

If you have more than twenty-five students in your class, modify the game by using three teams for each round instead of two teams. Or, if you have a very small group, it's OK to have one person on a team, or you might want to eliminate the studio audience and play only one round.

FOR STARTERS

10 to 15 minutes

FORGIVENESS FEUD

When students have arrived, have them form two groups. Then have one group form two teams while the other group sits together on the floor as the "studio audience."

Say: Let's start off today by playing a game. Our studio audience will have a very important role in the game today, and everyone will have a chance to be on a team and be part of the audience. I'll briefly describe a situation to our first two teams, and then I'll ask them a

question. Each team will have ten seconds to decide on an answer, write the answer on an index card, and bring the card to me.

Give each team three index cards and a pen or pencil, and ask each team to choose a team member to be the "runner." Then **say:**

> **While teams are deciding on their answers, each member of the studio audience will think about what his or her answer would be. After the teams have turned in their index cards, I'll read their answers to our audience. Audience, think about each answer carefully, decide which one is most like the answer you would have given, and then vote for that answer. The team that turned in the answer with the most audience votes gets a point. After three questions, the teams and the studio audience will switch places. Does everyone understand?**

When everyone is clear on the rules of the game, **say:**

> **OK, teams, here's your first situation: A boy accidentally steps on his dog's tail. The dog bites him. What does the boy do to the dog?**

After about ten seconds, ask the runner for each team to turn in the first index card. Shuffle the two cards, and then **say:**

> **Let's find out what our audience survey reveals.**

Read both answers to the audience. Then read each answer again, and ask students to raise their hands to vote for the answer most like the answer they would have given. Remind the audience that each person must vote but may vote only once. Then **say: Survey says...,** say aloud the audience's choice, and award a point to the team with that answer. Continue this pattern with the next two questions:

- **Your best friend is invited to the most incredible party of the year, and you ask her if you can go with her. She tells you she's going with some new friends and you'll have to find some other losers to spend Friday night with. What do you say to your friend?**
- **Your cousin is killed in a car accident by a drunk driver, who is then sentenced to three years in prison. After the three-year term, you see the driver again. What do you tell him?**

Have the audience applaud for the teams. Then continue with the game by having the audience form two teams and the original teams sit down as the audience. Give three index cards and a pen or pencil to each new team, and have teams choose runners. Play the game as before, using these questions:

- **Your baby brother finds your favorite baseball card on the floor in your room and proceeds to chew the card to a soggy pulp. What do you do?**

FYI

It's OK if teams give vague answers or answers that don't have anything to do with forgiveness. Any answer will prompt discussion later.

NOTES

- **Someone at school steals ten dollars from your locker. When you find out who did it, what do you say to her?**
- **Your friend confides to you that his older brother molested him when he was little. The next time you see your friend's brother, what do you do?**

Have the audience applaud for the teams, then prompt teenagers to form groups of five to **discuss** the following questions:

- **In our game show, were any questions harder to answer than the others? Why or why not?**
- **How did your responses vary with the different situations?**
- **What does it mean to forgive?**
- **How would you feel about forgiving the various wrongdoers from our game show situations? Why?**
- **What makes forgiveness easy or difficult?**

In their groups, have students read Isaiah 55:7 and then **discuss** the following questions:

- **What does this verse say about forgiveness? about God's ability to forgive?**
- **Do you think God's ability to forgive varies from situation to situation? Why or why not?**
- **Do you think God can forgive anyone for anything? Explain.**

Say: For us, forgiving someone may be an easy task or a difficult task, depending on the situation. Many of us have been hurt deeply by things others have said or done to us—and we need to find healing from those situations. We also need to reach the point of offering forgiveness to those who have hurt us.

Likewise, some of us may have done the hurting—we may have said or done things to others that were very wrong. God can offer forgiveness for those things too. With Jesus, God promises not only to forgive us but also to forget our sin.

THE POINT

God can provide healing and forgiveness for past hurts. God can forgive anyone, but often we need his help to forgive ourselves for things we've done or to forgive people who hurt us. Let's explore this issue further.

BIBLE TRUTH

20 to 25 minutes

CHAT ROOM

Line up two rows of chairs back-to-back in the middle of the room. Have students sit in the chairs, and distribute pens or pencils. **Say:**

> **Sometimes talking with other people on the Internet feels comfortable because we can join in conversations anonymously. We're going to create our own "chat room" to talk more about forgiveness. First, to get into the chat room, everyone will need to make up a "screen name."**

Give students a few seconds to create pseudonyms they can use to sign their responses. Encourage teenagers to use screen names that they haven't used before and that won't identify them.

After teenagers have created screen names, **say:**

> **Now let's go "online." I'm not going to ask you to reveal personal information, and you don't have to say or do anything you don't want to. When you receive the first message, read it and write a response. Try to disguise your handwriting so you retain your chat-room anonymity. Here's the first message.**

Give each student a copy of Message 1 from the "NetTalk" handout (p. 46), and give everyone one minute to read it and respond by writing on the handout (using disguised handwriting). When students are finished writing, **say:**

> **Now you're going to send your message. Sign your screen name, fold the paper in half, and pass it to your left until I say "stop."**

After about fifteen seconds, have each student stop, open the message, read it, and add a response. Remind students to continue signing their screen names to their responses. Have teenagers send the messages again by folding and passing the papers. Then **say:**

> **Wait! Another message is coming over the 'Net.**

Have students fold up their Message 1 slips and place them on the floor. Then distribute Message 2 to students, and have students continue to write responses and send them. Repeat the process with the third message. Each message should circulate to at least three students, but you can have teenagers circulate them more if time allows.

Once students have finished circulating the third message,

***FYI**

If you choose to modify this activity in any way, be sure to retain the elements of anonymity and separateness. Because the issue of sexual victimization is so personal and possibly emotional, students need to process the information with some privacy. They also need to feel the protection anonymity provides.

***FYI**

You can add variety to this activity by having teenagers switch directions as they pass their messages or having them pass their messages overhead to the people behind them. Be sure students pass their messages quickly and frequently so they can't figure out who the messages they receive came from. Also, be sure all teenagers have the same color ink or lead to write with so their writing won't be identified.

NOTES

have them form groups of four. Give each person a Bible, and have groups read Genesis 37:18-28; 50:15-21; and Luke 15:11-32.

After they're done reading, have groups **discuss** these questions:

- **How were the victims in these passages like the victims of sexual abuse or mistreatment we read about online? How were they different?**
- **Do you think Joseph and the father in the parable found it easy to forgive?**

Say: Sexual victimization can take many forms, such as sexual abuse or rape. It can also be more seemingly "minor" things like sexual harassment—comments or actions made towards a person that make him or her feel uncomfortable, sexually stereotyped, or pressured to participate in sexual acts.

Ask:
- **Do you think a victim of sexual abuse or harassment can or should forgive the offender? Why or why not?**
- **What are the advantages to forgiving someone? the disadvantages?**
- **In these Scripture passages, how did God treat the victims? the offenders?**
- **What were the consequences of the offenders' sins?**
- **Do you think forgiving an offender relieves him or her of the sin's consequences?**
- **Do you think God forgave the offenders in these stories? Explain.**

Say: Sometimes the hardest thing to do is to forgive yourself for things you've done in the past.

Ask:
- **Based on these stories, why is it important for someone to forgive himself or herself for wrongs from the past?**
- **Do you think God can forgive a sexual abuser?**
- **Do you think God can help us to forgive those who've hurt us? How?**
- **Do you think God can help us forgive ourselves if we may have sinned sexually or sexually victimized others in the past?**

Say: God can provide healing and forgiveness for past hurts. God can forgive anyone, and God wants us to forgive others, too. With God's help, the process of forgiveness can be easier. But it is still a process—sometimes a long, difficult, painful process. THE POINT

LIFE APPLICATION

15 to 20 minutes

FORGIVENESS TRAIL

Have teenagers gather in the area where you put the masking tape trail. **Say:**

This masking tape line represents the process of forgiveness and healing; as you can see, it's very complicated. Get into groups of four so you'll have some support. Each of you think about a situation in which someone needs forgiveness. You can think of your own situation, you can use the sexual victimization situations we read about in our chat room, or you can use a situation from our game show.

With your group, think of a creative way to travel together. The only rule is that you have to all be connected— for example, linking elbows, in a single file line with everyone hanging on to the person in front of him or her, or two people riding piggyback. In your group, follow the masking tape line until you reach a number written on the tape. Then find the piece of newsprint hanging on the wall that corresponds to that number. Still with your group, go to the newsprint, read it, and write a sentence reflecting what that step would be like in the situation you're thinking of. When everyone in your group is finished writing, go back together to the trail and continue until you get to the next number. Continue with this process until you reach the end of the line. Is everyone ready?

Have students line up with their groups; then **say:**

When we're on the trail of forgiveness, we may feel alone. The process can be long and difficult, but God is always with us. Let's begin the process with prayer.

Pray aloud:

Dear God, we know that you can provide healing and forgiveness for past hurts. It's hard for us sometimes to be forgiving of ourselves or others. Please help as we struggle to forgive those who have hurt us. Thank you for your loving grace and your strength. Amen. THE POINT

Send the first group of teenagers on the trail. As soon as a group has finished at the first station, send a new group. After every group has finished, have everyone cheer their success and then

*FYI

Are you concerned that one of your students may be a victim of sexual abuse? If so, do not hesitate to act. The first step is prayer. Next, find out if your church has a policy for handling this type of situation and follow that protocol. If your church doesn't have a policy, don't try to handle the situation on your own; contact a qualified Christian counselor or sex abuse prevention organization for guidance about how to proceed.

turn to each of their group members and tell them how they helped them through the process. Then have the whole class **discuss** the following questions:

- **What was it like to start the forgiveness trail by asking for God's help?**
- **What did you like or dislike about having people travel with you?**
- **What was the hardest stage? the easiest?**
- **Do you think God forgives in the same way we forgive?**

Say: God is infinitely wiser than we are. He loves us completely and extended the ultimate in grace to his people through Jesus Christ. No matter what we've been through sexually—whether we've been victimized, abused, harassed, or if we've done things to others that we regret—God can provide forgiveness and healing. He can be your guide as you go through the process of forgiving others or forgiving yourself.

THE POINT

BONUS ACTIVITY

up to 5 minutes

If you have time, try this Bonus Activity to close the study.

Pass out a strip of construction paper to each student and **say:**

You've just had a chance to walk the trail of forgiveness in groups. Yet for many of you that may not have been enough. You may need to walk that trail alone—to really deal with something on your own, between you and God.

Pass out the stapler and invite students to attach their paper strip around their ankle or wrist like a shackle. **Say:**

Our past hurts can keep us in bondage—they can feel like chains. We may be chained by our own feelings of guilt. We may be chained by feelings of hatred or bitterness toward someone who has hurt us. We need God's help to break free.

Encourage students to wear their shackles home and then to set aside time that evening to be alone with God and talk with him openly and honestly about their need for healing and forgiveness. Encourage them to tear off their paper shackles at the end of their prayer time, symbolizing the freedom God desires to give them through forgiveness.

Net Talk: Message 1

I feel so guilty. I try to ignore it, but it keeps haunting me. For the past few months, when my girlfriend and I were messing around, I was pressuring her to go farther...to have sex. I knew she didn't want to—but it was like something took over and I wasn't myself. Two weeks a she gave in. She didn't want to do it. I don't think she liked it, and she's seemed depressed ever since. I feel like a total jerk. I don't think I c ever forgive myself. I don't think God would ever forgive me either. Any advice?

—Marv2(

Net Talk: Message 2

I think I'm going to quit the soccer team. I love the sport, but I hate going to practice. The assistant coach makes me feel totally uncomfortable. He always gives me weird looks—sexual looks—and he won't leave me alone. Last week he pulled me aside and said I have nice legs. He always tries to hug me too. It's just no normal, the way he treats me. I can't stand being around him. To be honest, I hate him. He makes me feel...dirty. But whenever I think I'm ready to tell my mom about it, I feel too ashamed. What should I do?

--Worldcupchick

Net Talk: Message 3

One of my dad's old friends started sexually molesting me when I was little—probably four or five. I went on for a few years until I finally told my parents. The abuse ended and the man was arrested. M parents sent me to counseling. But now, even though it's been over for years, I can't forget the pain. Sometimes I feel completely ashamed. Sometimes I hate myself. I'll never be able to date or ge married like normal people—why would anyone want me? I'll never forgive him for what he did to me. What would you do?

—Bookwurm92

CHANGED 4 LIFE

Making good sexual choices isn't easy for teenagers! Help remind students of all that they've learned during these studies and celebrate their commitments by hosting a special event for parents and teenagers, such as a formal dinner or a pizza party. In addition to inviting parents, considering inviting other members of the church family who can support the teenagers, such as members of the pastoral staff, older siblings or college students, or even senior adult members of the church.

Make photocopies of the commitment section at the end of the "Dating Steam-Meter" handout (p. 25) to place at each table setting. Present a brief devotion during the dinner, encouraging teenagers to stick with God's plan for sex. Thank parents for their investment in their children and suggest ways they can encourage their teenagers as they navigate the rough terrain of peer pressure and sexual urges. Arrange for a few teenagers to share from their own lives during the dinner, highlighting how God has helped them grow in their understanding of sexuality during the four Bible studies.

Conclude the get-together by pointing out the commitment placard at each place setting, explaining that teenagers signed this commitment during one of the Bible studies. Congratulate the students on their commitment to be obedient to God, and prompt the adults at each table to take a few minutes to pray for the teenagers present, asking God to strengthen them in their commitment.